Act Like A Parent, Think Like A School Superintendent:

Information They Will Never Tell You

by

Dr. Mary L. Young

Act Like A Parent, Think Like A School Superintendent: Information They Will Never Tell You

Published by Dr. Mary L. Young

DEDICATION

This book is dedicated to my three sons Timothy, Nigel, and Gabriel. May all of your dreams come true!

TABLE OF CONTENTS

Chapter 1: My Why

When I think about parents being empowered, it excites me! Being empowered means that you are equipped with the necessary tools to make informed decisions for your children at school. Having power also means that you are aware of your rights and you exercise it to ensure that your children receive a high-quality education. What's interesting is that everyone in the educational setting doesn't share that same philosophy. In fact, after reading the title of this book, some educators may think that I have switched sides. As if I have betrayed the educational profession and somehow crossed the imaginary line of loyalty to the parent side.

However, my question to those educators is, why must there be sides? Where is it written that it's parents versus educators? At the end of the day, both parties should have the same goal: students. As a result, our priority should be the students and their success. If that is correct, then we should want our parents to be informed about the educational setting.

Most parents don't understand the current ebbs and flows of school life. Yes, you are participating in the Parent Teacher Association (PTA) and attend school functions. We love to see you there! However, your attendance only represents less than one percent of the total time your child is in school. Think about it, if your child attends school for seven hours a day in a 180-day school calendar year, that's 1,260 hours. If you were to attend every school function throughout the entire year, that would be about 25 hours. At most, you would have graced the school doors about two percent of the total time that your child is at school.

When you are not at your child's school, the other 98% percent of time is comprised of a lot of activities that you will never see and/or experience. Although you may ask your child what he/she learned and did at school that day, that information only scratches the surface of the school environment. In addition, the information that you receive is through the lens of a child, which means that there could be other factors that were missed in their recollection of events.

It's always interesting to talk to parents when their child has come home after an "eventful commotion", otherwise known as a fight, at school. Depending on the child's motivation, angle view, or memory, the description could have a wide range of variances. This is not to say that the child isn't telling the truth. You see, truth is relative. If the child believes that their perception is correct, he/she will adamantly stand by it. That's why schools have witnesses and cameras to assist them during investigations. Similar to a courtroom's list of witnesses to corroborate a case, the testimonies provide evidence in order for the jury or judge to make an informed decision.

As a parent you want to support your children, but sometimes you may lack the knowledge and understanding of the school dynamics. Although you were once a student many moons ago and can possibly relate to the school environment, things have definitely changed since your time in school. The days of the typewriter and floppy disk have been replaced with personal laptops and SMART boards.

Yes, things have definitely changed since your time in school. Educational jargon and initiatives have changed; from phonics to whole language, turnaround schools to transformation schools; it's not the same. Elementary schools even have a new way to teach addition and multiplication. Not only have the names changed, the protocols and policies have changed as well. With each new President of the United States of America in office, there is an appointment of a new Secretary of Education in the United States Department of Education, whose philosophical perspectives are at times the polar opposite of his/her predecessor. In an effort to stay abreast of the latest research, educators are constantly participating in an array of trainings to ensure students are learning and successful in the classroom. What was taught in the 1980s, 1990s, and now 2020s are worlds apart. With the evolving laundry list and constant movement of information, it's enough to drive any parent up the wall. By the time you have an understanding of the school's "new program" it has already changed to something else. Let me be clear, you are not crazy so exhale!

The Analogy

I recall needing my vehicle repaired and took it to the car dealership in my area. Normally, I was accustomed to my dad fixing it. As a skilled mechanic, he could easily identify the issue and rectify it. I also enjoyed the perk of it being free as well. However, once I moved away from home, the distance made it impossible for me.

In an effort to ensure that I was getting reputable service, I researched several locations in my area on the internet. Based on the company's ratings and customer comments, I made my selection. After all, I believed that my due diligence would pay off.

With optimism, I arrived at the dealership. There must have been an imaginary sign over my head that said "green alert" as I walked through the doors. Unbeknownst to me, my naive facial expression caused my repair bill to have additional zeros. What I thought was a simple repair turned into an itemized list that filled several pages. It appeared that my vehicle's issue had been multiplied by five. If I didn't know any better, you would have thought that my vehicle was on its last leg based on their diagnostic.

In an effort to verify the information that they provided to me, I reached out to my father. As I explained their analysis of the problem and the surmounting costs, I was quite surprised. He informed me that a lot of the information was incorrect. In fact, what was needed to repair my vehicle was rather simple and the cost was minimal. The additional charges on my vehicle repair estimate weren't necessary but a way for dealership to make more money by exaggerating the issue.

What's interesting is that the shop's employee presented the information with a high degree of confidence. As I asked questions, he provided a plausible rationale that appeared to make sense to me. So much so, that I almost questioned my father. However, knowing that my father was a proficient mechanic, I became a little bothered by the dealership's employee. I was upset because they were trying to take advantage of my limited knowledge of vehicles. They didn't care about its impact to me because it meant more money in their pockets and quotas filled for the month. Even more, this was someone who innocent people also found trustworthy because as customers, we believed that they would be honorable.

As I reflect on that experience, I think about the educational system. Similar to the employee at the car dealership, parents trust educators to tell them the truth and to do the right thing. You believe that schools are here to educate your children. When you bring your children to us, you have unwavering confidence that the teachers and school leaders will do what's best.

Unlike the car dealership, parents won't lose money when they enroll their children in school. However, there are decisions every day that occur within the four walls of the school that impact your children. Not from the aspect of abuse, mistreatment, or neglect but in power. Many of you are forfeiting rights and privileges, which could have a long-lasting impact on the future of your children.

Perspective

As an educator for almost 30 years, I have witnessed stellar educators, who work tirelessly to meet the needs of students. Although they are exceptional teachers & school leaders, there are far too many decisions that parents leave up to them to decide in regards to their children. As a result, some educators may form a negative opinion about parents. If you don’t believe me, look at your school’s climate survey from the teacher's perspective. They believe that a parent's lack of engagement means that they aren't concerned or care about their child's education. If you took the time to review the results, you are probably thinking, are they serious? What are those decisions? No one has informed me that there were options for my child.

From my vantage point, I don't see the actions of parents as you forfeiting your rights to the school. It appears that you aren't aware of it to make decisions on behalf of your children. Think about it. Do you know your child's rights or parental rights in the school system? What's interesting is the number of decisions that school districts frequently make that could make or break the trajectory of your children. Yet, you know nothing about.

As a parent, you have known your children from birth to 12th grade, yet you trust an educator, who has only known your child for one year at best to solely make life decisions. I'll restate the previous sentence in mathematical terms: 216 months (parent knowledge of your child) versus 10 months (teacher knowledge of your child). Yet, somehow the teacher is making the decision concerning your children. You are probably thinking, well, the educators have gone to college, majored in education, and know their craft. My response to you is absolutely. You are correct! However, to what degree do they know your child? With an average class size of 25 students, how long do you think it takes for a teacher to get to know a student? For many, by the time they begin to truly understand the personality and quirks of your children, its halfway through the school year. Even then, it's plausible that they may still not know your child. Although this may be new information to you, it's better to learn it sooner than later.

In fact, decisions about your child's education are made each day. Many times, you don't know the impact that those changes will have on your children. You look up and you know that something is different, but you don't know what to ask or who to talk to. Some parents become disengaged not because you don't care about your child's education, you just don't know what to do. Other parents become frustrated by the lack of clarity. You probably believe that not knowing the topic may make you look foolish to the school staff and so you allow the school to make the decision for your children. Please don't let your lack of knowledge or clarity to stop you. I am here to help you because your children need you. You are their biggest champion and advocate. No one will speak up for them more than you!

School Situation

A parent called me about a situation in her son's school. It was during the 2020-2021 school year and school was closed as a result of the pandemic. In his now new reality of virtual school in the first grade, his mother logged him into class every morning to receive instruction from his teacher. As the weeks progressed, the mother noticed that her son was being marked absent. When she reached out to the teacher to inquire about the absences, she was informed by the teacher that her son hadn't participated in class. In response, the mother informed her that her son was in attendance every day. To which the teacher replied that he never participated in class. As a result of her not hearing him speak, she marked him absent.

When the mother informed me of her plight and asked for my assistance, I asked her an array of questions to get an understanding because in my mind clearly something was missing in the story. After hearing all of the information, it was apparent that her son's silence was causing him to be marked absent in school. What's interesting is that the student was physically present in the teacher's classroom from August to March, until schools transitioned to virtual learning. Had she not realized by then that the student was an introvert? In fact, he speaks with a very soft, low monotone voice. So low that you may have to ask him several times to repeat himself just to understand what he is saying to you. Had she not observed this behavior in class? Surely in the small group reading, he was asked to speak and she noticed it. In addition, which school policy allowed a present student to be marked absent because he didn't participate in virtual class? If it were a new policy, were the parents informed of the impact to their child's attendance and grades? While we'll never know what was really going on in the classroom, our focus was on the present issue, the student. We wanted him to be successful in the classroom.

Although there were a number of steps that I provided the parent, one major recommendation was to have a conference with the teacher to discuss her son's learning style and temperament. During the conversation, the mother informed the teacher that her son was an introvert. In addition, I was able to guide the parent on how to properly advocate for her son. As a result, the parent further explained to the teacher how her son learned and provided her with strategies to ensure her son participated in class, such as call his name to participate. As a parent, she would encourage her son to speak in class because this was a home-school partnership. It wasn't about who was right or wrong. It was about what was best for her son. In the end, everything worked out for all parties. However, I'm sure that in other classrooms around the nation, there were situations similar to this one that were never resolved by parents, and unfortunately the students suffered as a result of it. This should never be the case!

Communication Matters

I told you the previous story because events like these are very common in schools. This is a direct result of miscommunication. Please know that schools are not intentionally trying to mislead you. What's interesting is schools send home tons of communication to parents. From emails to voice messages to newsletters, the list goes on and on. From the school's perspective, they believe that they have done their job by keeping parents abreast of the school activities. However, there is a disconnect because some parents don't see it that way.

When schools convey information to parents, do they also inform you of its purpose? Are parents aware of its impact or consequences? While most school leaders believe that the frequency of communication is what parents are seeking, could this be seen as information overload? Honestly speaking, there have been times when I became annoyed because the emails or recorded calls had nothing to do with my child. It was for those students who rode bus number 455 or the students who were played volleyball. When messages like this frequently happen, many parents don't bother listening to any of the messages because they believe that the information won't apply to them. As a result, you become accustomed to not listening to school messages and you end up missing the important ones and deadlines.

I recall a funny information overload story that I heard several years ago. One Sunday a woman attended service at her church. As she was exiting the building, her pastor greeted her and asked if she had enjoyed the message. In response, she informed him that the information was great but it was too much to hear in one sitting. She suggested that he should chunk size the information to allow members to easily digest and understand it. To which he replied that his lengthy sermons were due to the sporadic service attendees. His goal was to "get it all in" while he had them in service because he didn't know when they would return again. After hearing his heartfelt response, she graciously informed him about life on their farm.

On some days the cows graze in the field and eat the herbs. However, in order to ensure that they receive the proper nutrition, they feed them bales of hay. Although the cows infrequently come into the pasture to eat, when they finally come in, we don't dump the truckload of hay on them at one feeding. For some cows eating too much hay reduces their performance and sometimes lead to death. As she completed her story of life on the farm to her pastor, in response he nodded with a big smile because he too, got the message.

If your child's school sends multiple messages a day to parents, they are dumping the barrel of hay on you. If you receive a call, text and email from central office, and a reminder of the previous message from your children's schools, you just received a barrel of hay. If you received a 100-page student handbook from each of your children's schools and you were asked to read, sign, and return it the next day, it looks like you may have a barrel of hay.

Meaningful Communication - What's interesting about the parent mode of communication that some schools use, is that it isn't a best practice. In the school world, a best practice is a strategy or technique that a teacher uses in the classroom that is research-based. In order to be called a best practice, there must be evidence of its optimal effectiveness above other methods among a large number of classrooms.

In the classroom, one best practice that teachers use daily with students is to communicate the rationale or purpose of the lesson. Before the lesson is taught, the teacher informs the students of the lesson objective, purpose of the lesson, activities, and assignment. Why do teachers do this? Because students are always asking where will they use what they have learned in the classroom? As a result, they are informed why it is important for them to know the information. In addition, the teacher informs the class how the new information could be used in the real world. This helps students to make a connection to the information, it increases the student engagement, and mastery of the lesson.

Similarly, schools should do the same for parents by differentiating information. First, by only providing parents with applicable information. You don't need to hear about the bus that is running late on the opposite side of town at 5:30am. Secondly, inform parents of the purpose for the information and how it may impact their child or the school. You may need to know that failure to return the lunch form could result in your child not receiving free lunch. If your child's school isn't implementing meaningful strategies like the examples above, you have a right to ask. When parents receive essential communication and understand its purpose, you are able to be more engaged with the school. These small awareness bricks lay the foundation to a healthy home-school partnership. In order for this to occur, parents and teachers must collaborate to understand the whole child and meet his/her academic needs in school. As a parent, your voice matters!

In the best-case scenario, if you remain silent and your child has made the honor roll, you don't bother to ask questions because you are pleased with the grades. In the worst-case scenario, you have been officially notified in December that your child is in danger of falling his/her grade for the school year and you don't know what to do. Wherever you may find yourself as a parent, the fact still remains the same, healthy dialogue between the home and school are critical.

I'm just wondering what would happen if an educator, who knew their content, aligned with a parent, who knew their children? How much farther could your children be, if you partnered with your child's teacher at the beginning of the school year? Yes, he/she made the honor roll. However, what if I told you that there was so much more? As opposed to B's, how would you feel if he/she could make all A's and enroll in advanced classes? What about graduate high school with a high school diploma and an associate's degree? For some students, this is a reality. If it's not occurring at your child's school, please know that it is possible. In order to get the ball rolling, it starts with you simply starting the conversation.

Rationale for Blueprint

As an educational advocate for parents and students, over the years parents have come to me for advice regarding their children. Why, because they trust me. They know that although I am an educator, I am a parent first. Also, I will provide them with an informed response so they can make the best decision for their children. This is my reason for writing this book because I know that there are other parents who wish they had someone to help them too.

Athletic coaches have a playbook of strategies as a guide to teach their players. They not only teach these plays; they watch videos after each game to determine its effectiveness. In order for the players to implement these strategies with precision, they have to understand the field (landscape). They must know the team's makeup by knowing all of the positions on the team. Are they offensive or defensive players? Is the person a quarterback or lineman? Each player has in depth knowledge of the rules of the game and plays because they have the playbook.

Parents, this book is your educational blueprint. This guide will allow you to leverage the educational system to ensure your children's success. In order for your children to win in this ever-changing school world, you have to know how to play the game. You can't afford to idly sit on the sidelines as a spectator because you are a player in this game. Although you may be new to this process, I am your official cheerleader. My goal will be to enthusiastically encourage and support you.

Through my lens as a former teacher, school administrator, and school Superintendent, you will have the home team advantage because I know the facilities, the fans, and the rules. This information will help you to navigate your children's school district. By the end of this book, you will be an empowered parent. The purpose is not to arm you to fight but rather to engage your children's school system on equal ground. The strategic plays listed in this book coupled with your knowledge of your child will ensure a definite win for your children!

Chapter 2: The Art of War in School

One day my high school son came home upset because of an incident at school, and he wasn't pleased with the results. During the course of a conversation with his teacher at lunchtime, he believed that her response wasn't exactly correct, and it rubbed him the wrong. However, since elementary school, he was always taught to tell his father or I if he had a problem with an adult at school so that we could resolve the issue adult to adult. Well, it must have been a blood moon the prior night because on this particular day, all bets were off and there was a major shift in his energy. Apparently, he had selective amnesia and chose to take matters in his own hands. Although the information that he conveyed to his teacher was correct, it was not palatable coming from a student. How dare a student tell her that she was wrong? The nerve of him. As a result, the teacher called me to report the incident.

When my son arrived home from school, I informed him of the phone conversation. As we discussed the incident in full detail, I could visibly see the indignation rise up in his body. From my son's perspective, he believed that he was advocating for himself. He wanted the teacher to have the facts in order to make an informed decision. However, she appeared to be more concerned with his approach as opposed to the accuracy of the information. From the teacher's perspective, my son should have stayed in a child's place, regardless, and complied with her instructions.

As we discussed and compared the varying perspectives of the teacher and his, he became even more frustrated during the conversation. He recalled a recent occasion when I had informed him that as a young man in high school, he had a voice and should express himself. Our goal, as parents, was to teach him how to advocate for himself. We didn't want him to shrink or not give a response when he needed to stand up for himself. However, he was now confronted with an encounter that left him bewildered because the one time that he used his voice at school with an adult, he felt like he was being muted.

As I looked at my son's defeated face and heard the anguish in his voice, I realized that it was time to teach him how to play the game. We discussed the principles from the book, The Art of War, by Sun Tzu. Due to his level of engagement and curiosity, I provided him with an eBook copy. Then I emailed him a brief summary and specific quotes that aligned to the interaction with his teacher.

To my amazement, he was easily able to grasp and align the book's concepts to the incident at school. In that moment, for the first time, he was introduced to the art of war in school. After he recognized the interaction for what it was, his angst slowly disappeared because it all made sense to him. As he identified his teacher (the player), her role (power), and plays (actions), his enlarged bright eyes glistened like a flashlight being turned on in a dark room. This was his first lesson on warfare in the school setting and he understood that being equipped with the necessary skills would lead him to win the war, although he had lost this battle. He understood that one component of losing this battle meant that he had to fix the tension between him and his teacher. In addition, he also understood that the lost was due to how he delivered the information and the timing of the school year. It was the last month of school and further engaging the matter wasn't worth it because school would be over in a couple more weeks. In addition, he was aware of the teacher's bitter interactions when other students crossed her path in previous months. Based on that analysis, he identified action steps that he would take to resolve the matter. That evening he emailed the teacher an apology explaining his enlightenment. In an effort to seal the deal, the next day after class, he spoke to the teacher to mend the relationship. In the end, he understood the bigger picture, win the war.

After reading how we handled the situation, you may have an array of questions and opinions. Let me be clear, I could have intervened and reacted with a heavy hand because of my expertise in the game. There are a number of strategies that I could have used that would have knocked the teacher on her back leaving her maimed and discombobulated. However, knowledge of the art of war, diverted me in another direction. Instead of exerting my time and energy, I decided to use this opportunity to teach my son a valuable lesson. As a result, he mastered his first lesson on the art of war in school.

At first glance, you may wonder why are we talking about a war in my children's school district? I'm not trying to fight anyone. Besides, there's enough violence already in the world. You are correct! The impact of gun violence has ravaged our country and schools. We don't need any more bloodshed in our schools or on our streets.

You may now be wondering, where are the strategies to the playbook that I spoke of in chapter 1? You are ready to learn the secrets of the school system. Where is the dirt? Where do you find the buried bodies? My response to your questions is to slow down and first receive the foundation. Did you know that the foundation in a house is the most important part? Similar to a house, if the foundation isn't properly secured, it will be hard to hold up the structure. Likewise, you not understanding certain principles of war may leave you exposed, cracked, and possibly crumbing in your attempts to support your children at school. As your official cheerleader, I'm rooting for you to win the war. However, you must first be prepared before you can start!

The Chinese military general, Sun Tzu, was not only a war leader but a successful strategist. As a philosopher, his enemies were conquered in his mind long before troops stepped on the battlefield. Thousands of years after his death, leaders still incorporate his wisdom in their practices. For example, when you hear people say that if you take out the leader in a group, the rest will fall in line; it comes from Tzu. When he was faced with the challenge of commanding order in the region, even against the king's desires, he made swift and precise moves. As a result, his respect and notability increased in the land.

In his book, The Art of War, he candidly conveys to the readers the dynamics of power and its impact, if you don't understand the elements around you. Although Tzu is talking about a physical war on a battlefield, many of the themes in his book are also applicable for you as a parent because there are school elements all around you that influence your child's school district. It is important for you to be able to navigate through the ambiguous school environment, while also avoiding the community landmines. In order to ensure your children's success, insight of the players and their roles is crucial to the game. In addition, you must possess the knowledge of how the players operate in and around the landscape.

In addition, being astute of their responsibilities and power is critical to your survival.

As a parent, it's important to know when to strike and when to go in peace. Doing this requires access and skills. Although this may have never crossed your mind, your children can be a casualty of school war. Yes, as a result of warring factions in your local community, your children's school could be innocently stuck in the middle. Understanding this landscape will aid you in how you do what you do and with whom. You need to have strategy to know when to duck and take cover. This knowledge is the bedrock to the strategies that leads to triumph.

Chapter 3: Your Landscape

In order to move around the school system as a parent, you must understand the unique characteristics of your school district's terrain. Although schools are in the business of educating students, just below its picturesque image lies suspense and uncertainty. For those of us who have witnessed its fury carry its psychological battle scars because deep inside the layers of the system of schools can be beastly. Yet, there are many educational warriors who remain vigilant and purpose-driven because we know that the future lives of our children are at stake. In order to gain new territory for the advancement of all children, we're fully aware that it comes with its share of opposition. Although as a parent, you'll never be touched by the horrors of its piercing cries, knowledge of the terrain enables you to assess the landscape of the school district and avoid the never-ending merry-go-round of frustrations and dead ends.

Questions to consider as you examine the school system landscape include:

- What do you know about your children's school district or school?
- How long has it been in existence?
- Have the school district's or school's demographics changed over the past thirty years? If so, how?
- How has this change impacted the school (quality of education, teachers, funding, etc.)?
- What are the conversations around rezoning or redistricting? Is it aligned to a certain socioeconomic status, race, or part of town?
- What are the adjectives associated with your children's school district or school?

After reading these questions, you are probably asking yourself, why did I purchase this book? Before you close this book and quit, I have the answers for you. Again, your cheerleader's got you! The answers to these questions can be found in several places on the internet, such as your county's historical website, the school district's "about us" page, the county's census report, and Wikipedia. For example, if you want to review the historical trends, Google the "(name of your county) census report".

The school district's historical landscape provides you with the background of the district. For example, the demographics in Washington, D.C. have drastically changed. In 1800, there were about fourteen thousand people, comprised of mostly White Caucasians. Although the numbers grew exponentially, White Caucasians remained the predominant race until 1990. After the 1990s for the first time in the history of D.C., the African-Americans (Blacks) outnumbered White Caucasians. In 2022, African-Americans (Blacks) still outnumber White Caucasians. However, based on the trends, White Caucasians may soon become the predominant race again because there is a shift. This shift is not only in race but in the socioeconomic status that impacts taxes and revenue, future government officials, and gentrification just to name a few.

Although I only provided you with the racial makeup trends of the District of Columbia, its impacts are far reaching. Intertwined in the data profile, the historical landscape determines the economic and social decisions in our local communities. All of these factors influence schools. They impact which schools receive more money and priority, while others are left to sink or swim. If you peel back the surface of your school district, you may see a high correlation between successful schools and highly effective, experienced teachers. Many of these decisions are influenced by empowered parents, who have already learned the game to advocate for their children. Although they have used their knowledge of the landscape to ensure their children receive a high-quality education, you have now entered the zone. And guess what? You will too!

Once you begin to observe patterns of imbalance in your school district, what will you do? The ability to observe is crucial because you must be able to see over a particular area to acquire targets. I liken this to a quarterback on a football field. When discussing the effectiveness of the play, many people refer to the quarterback's height, which allows him to see over the other players to view the entire field. Before he passes the football to his teammate, he assesses the field to determine the areas of weakness and strategizes which player is in the best position to reach the goal. Although there may be multiple players (targets), his vantage point allows him to easily see the best option.

Recognition is important and knowing where to focus your attention is also crucial. Based on the identification of observed practices in the school district, what will be your target? Who will you talk to about your concerns? Do they have the power to change the situation? Before you can bring real change to your school district, you must understand the total picture.

The days of being loud and obnoxious at meetings are long gone. Yes, you can still do it. In fact, in many school districts across the nation parents receive thunderous applauses from the audience for their grandstanding. However, unbeknownst to you, this form of behavior is a turnoff to some school district employees and board members. Although your polarizing speech may garner support and an investigation will be completed, those antics only yield a temporary fix. When the crowds have gone home, what do you really have left as proof that your actions made a difference for your children? In an effort to have a sustainable goal, it requires more than just a bullhorn. You need strategy!

Chapter 4: Your Players

The players are the people and groups in the district's ecosystem on the landscape. I liken the school district's ecosystem to mother nature because it represents the vast diversity in our communities that all work together. What's interesting about nature is that the greater the biodiversity, biological diversity, the more resistant it is in the face of adversity. In essence, nature has recognized its extensive, multi-faceted factors and discovered that this it is necessary in order to be sustain life. What's fascinating is that mother nature has ascertained that it's stronger together than apart. Although we are considered the most intelligent species on earth, nature has become a role model of how we should all work together, regardless of our differences.

The school district's organisms in the ecosystem are referred to as the stakeholders, such as but not limited to the businesses, government officials, Board of Education members, school district employees, parents/grandparents, and students. They contribute to the life of the community, its evolution and culture because they have a vested interest. Although there are no written rules in the transfer of energy to survive, some may say that life in the school district's landscape is composed of the primary producer (parents and students) being eaten by the consumer (community influencers) to gain power and dominance.

One of the biggest challenges to a community's ecosystem is adequate funding. Many times, local budget decisions are based on the voters. However, it is a known fact that certain age groups don't vote. In many places the largest percentage of voter participants are senior citizens. If they have to decide between lowering their taxes due to having a fixed income versus increasing the taxes for school funding, what do you think will happen? Yes, schools will lose every time because our senior citizens don't have any children in the school system so they aren't personally impacted by the school district's plight. On the other hand, this is not to say that we should make costs unbearable for our seniors and disperse all of the money to the future generations. Although we see these dynamics in our communities, who is having conversations about the possible options? Who said that it had to be one or the other? Without communication and a desire to find a resolution, there will be a continual battle and someone will always come up short.

Local Government Officials

The local government officials include people such as the county executive, county commissioner, and mayor. As an elected office, they are given the power to manage a specific geological region, such as counties, towns, parishes, and regions. In addition, they are responsible for allocating funds to ensure that the school district operates efficiently each school year. Once the federal government assigns funds to the state, the state allocates funds to the local jurisdiction who then assigns funds to the school district. If one of those funneling agencies has a financial challenge, it is very likely that the school district will be impacted by it.

Overall, the school district's budget is a combination of money from the county, state, and federal based on its student demographics and programs/initiatives. Many people may not realize this small fact but the taxes, such as property and income, received by the county's residents determine the amount of money that schools will receive each year. So, if the majority of your county's residents have a low socioeconomic status, it impacts how much money is given to the school district. In addition, where you reside also has a huge impact on the educational system and available services for your children. For example, the higher priced homes are taxed more and the lower priced homes are taxed less because of the value assessment fees.

After reading this process many of you may have concerns. Various questions may arise, such as:

- How do you break the cycle of low income school districts receiving limited funding, yet they are expected to meet the same goals as other school districts?

- How does a low income school district recruit the best teachers with the lowest salary in the region?

- How does a low income school district meet the needs of all learners when the state implements a limit on fully funding certain student groups?

- What are the necessary conversations that your community must have with the elected officials?

- How do you lobby your local government to address your concerns?

Board of Education

By federal law, every school district and charter school are designated as a Local Education Agency (LEA). Each LEA is governed by a Board of Education. Most Board of Education members are elected but there are some boards that have appointed members. The board size generally ranges from five to eleven members. Every board has a chair/chairperson, who serves as the point of contact. In addition, the chair leads the board and facilitates the meetings. However, the chair is not the supervisor of the board because they all have equal rights. All members serve a four-year term. Similar to other elected officials, there is little to no criteria to become a board member. In most places, if you are a resident of the county and of legal age, you are eligible. So, if you have a desire to ensure student achievement in a safe and nurturing environment for all students, you may be an excellent candidate!

This position has a time commitment. Generally speaking, boards meet about three times a month and meeting times and the length varies by board. Most meetings start in the evening and may be anywhere from 30 minutes to several hours in length. Lastly, based on the state's school board association guidelines, members must attend a training to learn the roles and responsibilities of the position, as well as state regulations and policies.

Most Board of Education members are paid a monthly salary. There are about 15,000 school boards in the United States and the average salary for each member is about $25,000 per year. However, some boards, like Chicago Public Schools and New York City Schools aren't compensated, while L.A. Unified's board works full-time and makes over $100,000 a year. In addition to the salary, all of their district expenses, such as travel mileage, conferences, and lodging, are paid by the school district.

Have you ever wondered how a decision was made in the school district? As the governing body for the school district, boards have certain liberties on how the school system will function. Depending on your community's traditions, culture, and values, there are a wide variance of options that the board may chose to operate. Although most of their policies are guided by federal and state laws, there is still a great deal of autonomy that each school district has the power to exercise within their scope. For example, the Board of Education decides the district's goals and priorities, oversees the budget and approves the curriculum. Although the Superintendent makes recommendations to the board to complete certain actions, the final decision to move forward rests solely with the Board of Education.

In order to know your school district's policy, go to the Board of Education page on the school district's website. While you are there, review the most recent board meeting minutes. This information provides the agenda, documentation, and decisions. Each state has an Open Meeting Law, which requires the board to provide advance notice of the meeting to the public and allow the public to attend meetings. If the discussion is on private matters, such as individual students or staff, those meetings are closed to the public. This protects the rights of those individuals.

The following are questions that you may want to know about your school district's Board of Education members:

- Who are your school district's Board of Education members?

- Are they elected or appointed members?

- What was their motivation to become a Board of Education member?

- Do they have children or grandchildren who are enrolled in the school system? Yes, there have been incidences that board members have enrolled their children in schools outside of the district.

- Do they share your philosophies or know the predominant philosophy to make decisions for your children? If not, who do they represent and what are the implications?

- Is every board decision based on a "student-first" mindset?

- Are the board's decisions aligned with the strategic plan?

Unofficial Board of Education Members

These are the people in your community who have great influence. Influence doesn't always equate to wealth. These are the people who are well-known and respected in your district's ecosystem. Many times, they have done selfless acts to help others, such as back to school giveaways and Thanksgiving boxes. They have the ability to inspire and create camaraderie among varying sects of people because they use their knowledge of history and tradition to unite the community. When it's time to make decisions in the school district, people listen to them. Depending on the matter, their opinions could have a significant impact on the school system.

As a school Superintendent, I created an advisory for my influencers. This gave them a space to hear the school district's goals, plans, and needs. In addition, they were able to provide the strengths, weaknesses, obstacles, and threats from their perspective. This meeting provided us space to arm them with information about the school district. In addition, we were able to strengthen our plans based upon their feedback. In the absence of communication, imaginations soar, tensions may rise, and counterproductive realities are formed. This group was beneficial to reaching the school district's goals because it was inclusive of varying stakeholder feedback. One way to becoming an empowered parent includes joining the Superintendent's advisory. You not only have access to the unofficial board members, you have an opportunity to have a voice.

As a parent, you need to know who they are in your community. Board of Education members may refer to them as constituents. What's interesting is that everyone in the community is a constituent because of your residency. However, when that term is used by board members, most likely they are referring to the unofficial board members. You may easily identify them because they are probably your retired district employees (especially if a building was named after them or their picture is on the wall), faith-based leaders, community organization leaders, and civic volunteers. In addition to their identification, you want to know what's on their mind? What's their passion and mission? This doesn't mean that they may always agree with you. However, the more information that they have on an issue from you, broadens their perspective and possibly their actions.

School Superintendent

The school district's school Superintendent is the Chief Executive Officer, CEO, and reports to the Board of Education, not one individual board member. Although there are times when a singular board member may display an action that he/she is the sole supervisor of the Superintendent, this protocol is not supported by state regulations. The entire unit, all board members, act and serve as one voice. If there are seven board members, there is still one voice due to the voting results.

The Superintendent ensures the implementation of the Board of Education policies by creating protocols that may be referred to as Standard Operating Procedures (SOP). The Board of Education and the Superintendent work together to fulfill the mission and vision of the school district. Lastly, the superintendent has oversight of the school district's day-to-day operations and the long-range planning. If there are any district matters, the Superintendent is the appointed point person. As the senior leader, he/she designates specific duties and responsibilities to district staff and school principals due to the magnitude of the work.

School District Employees

There are two groups of school district employees: central office and school-based employees. Central office employees are located in an office building. While the position titles may vary by school district location and size, the Superintendent's leadership team, Executive Cabinet, oversees and manages the district's academics, finances, operations, and personnel of the school district. Under those leaders various personnel are assigned to assist in completing the scope of work. The purpose for the central office is to serve schools. In addition, they are a resource to schools to ensure they have what they need to educate all students. Without students there would be no schools and without schools, there would be no central office.

The other group of school district employees is schools, which is composed of the principal, teachers, and support staff. Some of the support staff include the secretaries, custodians, food nutrition workers, and teacher aides. All of the school employees work together to ensure the day-to-day duties of the school are seamless. From the custodians, who maintain a clean learning environment to the bus drivers, who safely transport students to school on time, like our fingers, each person serves a purpose and they are all essential.

personnel are assigned to assist in completing the [illegible] and fulfill the purpose for the central office [illegible] to serve schools. In addition, [illegible] resources schools [illegible] they have what they need to educate all students. [illegible] students [illegible] would be no schools [illegible] without schools [illegible] would be [illegible] central office.

In addition, many of school districts' employees [illegible] [illegible] teachers, and support staff [illegible] and [illegible] operational workers and bus drivers. All of these [illegible] [illegible] the [illegible] [illegible] environment [illegible] [illegible]

Chapter 5: Your Resources

Every organization, be it small or large, operates under an outlined standard of operation, which ensures order and efficiency in the organization. These tenets provide the framework for how the organization will do business. There is purpose in knowing your school district's information. As a parent, you want to know their mode of operation. How do they do what they do and why? Having knowledge of the school district's mode of operation provides you with the necessary information to know how they will interact with you, your children, and its employees. What good is it to have your children enrolled in a district and not know your rights or what your child should have access to? Although most school districts have similar initiatives and program, no two are alike. Also, knowing the school district's programs better equips you to advocate for your children.

As an empowered parent, there are several items that you need to have in your resource toolbox. Knowledge of these tools is another brick to your foundation to understanding the school district's protocols and procedures. In an effort to keep things simple, you will want to know how to navigate the school district's website. Using the website, you will want to locate the Board of Education's website & policies, the Strategic Plan, and the Student Parent Handbook.

Website

Every school district has established documents that are used to govern and implement their policies. Most, if not all of the information is provided on the district's website. If the documents are not on the school district's website, you have a right as a parent to request it.

In order to locate the various documents on the website, Google your school district's name on the internet. On the landing, home page, you may see an array of items. Staying focused on the specific section allows you to not become overwhelmed by the wealth of information and images. Each category has a heading title to describe the information that you will see in that section, followed by subheadings to group similar topics for your review. Most school districts will have pictures of students and employees as evidence of academic success. You may also see a calendar of the school district's upcoming events. If you scroll down to the bottom of that website page, you will see the school district's contact information and possibly a list of other items, which have been identified as the most used or requested information for its users. If at any time, you don't see the information that you need on the website, you may search for it using the search bar. Always remember to use the current school year in your search because previous versions of the document will also be listed and you want to review the most current information.

Board of Education Website & Policies

Before you review the Board of Education policy, there are a couple items that you may want to know first. On their website page, you will be able to view the pictures and the names of each member. Some school districts provide the biography of each member. Although this biography isn't necessary, it's great to know the background of each board member. Near each board member's picture, you will also see the position that they are serving, the year that their time on the board will end, and their contact information.

As you scroll through the page, you may see the board's meeting calendar that provides the date, time and location. Each school district may use various names to describe their meetings. The general rule of thumb is that if the title states, Board meeting, it is open to the public. The closed session or executive meetings are not available to the public because the topics involve people's personal information. For example, a student's appeal concerning disciple or an employee's contract. If you have any questions about the type of meeting and who can attend, you can always call the school district for additional information.

Another section on the board's website is for those who would like to speak at the board meeting or public hearing. By law you are allowed to address the Board of Education about any concerns. Depending on the number of participants, each person will have about three minutes. It is important that you know and follow the guidelines because failure to do so make result in you not being heard. In order to ensure your message is clear, you may want to write down what you are going to say and practice reading it to ensure you meet the time requirement.

The title, board docs, is the meeting agenda and documents. When you click on that link, you will see a couple headings. However, in an effort to stay focused, look for the title meetings. The meetings website page records all of the school district's previous and upcoming meetings. This section is useful if you want to know what the Board of Education discusses at the meetings. As you review the agenda, you will see the topics that will be or have been discussed. In addition, you are able to view the documents that were provided at the meeting for each board member. These documents are very important because it's what the board members use to make their decisions. To review these documents, look for the document icon next to the agenda topic.

Policies - Each school district's Board of Education must provide all stakeholders (the public) access to this manual. This electronic document averages about 1,000 pages, if you were to print it. Please don't become alarmed or try to print this entire document because policies are updated about every four months. Overall, the guidelines are very detailed and purposeful.

After you locate the Board of Education policies and headings, you will identify the various topics that are covered in that section, such as personnel, students, and instruction. Generally speaking, the policies are broken down into about nine categories. You may want to take about fifteen minutes to familiarize yourself with the categories and the topics in the categories. The federal and state regulations are identified with a specific coding that correlates to the governing federal or state statue. If the policy doesn't have a federal/state code, generally speaking, it is a policy that the board has full autonomy to make decisions on for the school district.

If you wanted to review the policies for students, click on the students' link. That page provides all of the protocols for how the district does business for students. If we were to look at the attendance policy, you will see guidelines outlined for you. It's important to note that all Board of Education members, school employees, students, and parents must comply with the policies. Failure to do so is a violation and subject to consequences.

Leveraging the Board of Education policies are pivotal because it is the great equalizer. Everyone is required to use it and abide by it. (Secret: No one in the school district knows the entire document verbatim because of its length.) One rule of thumb before attending any district meeting is to review the board's policy to ensure that you know the guidelines and you are able to speak to it. Unfortunately, there have been times when employees have conducted business that was contrary to the board's policies. If no one is verifying the information, you could be easily led astray.

For example, the attendance policy may say that students are assigned to a school based on safety, transportation, and school capacity. What this means is that the school district has the latitude to move students to another school. As a parent, you need to know what this means for your children. In response, you could ask:

- Why was the decision made? What were the factors?

- If the concern was transportation, could the student be a car rider and still attend the school?

- If the concern was building capacity, are there alternative classroom arrangements, such as combining grades or using a classroom modular?
- If there are siblings in the same school, what is the principal doing to keep the family together?

- If you can't remember any of these questions, always ask why? The school district owes you a reasonable answer in a timely manner.

Strategic Plan

The school district's strategic plan is the blueprint for the system's improvement. If you don't see the document on the home page, Google strategic plan and the school year (Example: strategic plan 2022) in the search bar. The strategic plan generally spans a five-year time period. Most strategic plans have about five areas of focus that are specifically aligned to the needs of the school district. The overarching goal is that if the school district works on these areas, it will become more effective and efficient, which will result in academic success for all students.

All strategic plans begin with the school district's vision and mission. These statements serve as the guide for the district. The vision of the school district informs stakeholders of the desired future for the system. It's an image of what the school district hopes to become. The mission statement lets you know their purpose for existing. For example, the mission of Dr. Mary L. Young County Schools is to prepare graduates to compete and succeed in a global society. This means that the school district's focus is to ensure that everything that they do prepares students be successful in the world. In order for students to graduate, they must master all of the standards in every grade to pass. This means that all teachers and grades matter. In addition to students graduating, the goal is for them to be successful in life. The interesting point about success is that it is relative. Some families may view getting a job after college as being a success. While others may view graduating high school and working at the local factory as being successful. Although both are considered commendable because students should be college and/or career ready, it is my belief that all students should be provided the appropriate education to decide their course. This means that as a parent, you want to make sure that your children are enrolled in courses that provides them options for college and career.

An empowered parent uses their voice to influence the direction of the school district's strategic plan. Did you know that during the course of your children's 13 years in school (K-12), the school district's mission, vision, and/or strategic plan could change every five to seven years? Imagine driving to Maryland, then you are told six years later that you have been rerouted and you are now headed to Kentucky. Then five years later you are told that you have been rerouted to Illinois. What if the majority of parents wanted to go to Florida? However, if no one had knowledge of this information because parents didn't share their desired outcome, the school district is headed to Illinois based on the minority of parent voices. Does this make sense to you? However, this happens in many school districts around the country. The question becomes, how do you change that?

They just sign the form. It is only after they have a problem at school, that they pick it up to review it. This is definitely not a good practice. I understand that you have a lot on your plate. However, when you and your children read the student handbook and understand it, this lessens the chances of you being called at work or asked to take time off from work to attend an unexpected meeting. Although it may seem like a lot, putting your reading time in at the beginning drastically decreases unwanted additional time at school. Simply put, when you and your children understand and comply with the student handbook, you avoid school drama.

As a parent, knowledge and understanding of the student handbook can also be used to leverage school decisions. I vividly recall a parent friend reaching out to me about her daughter. She had a received a phone call about an incident between her daughter and another student at school. As a result, the school leader decided to suspend her daughter. Because the empowered parent knew the student handbook "inside and out" she challenged the school's decision. Based on the student discipline infractions, the school leader had assigned her daughter a more punitive measure. Her daughter's actions warranted a lesser consequence. Although the school leader was upset, the decision was overturned because they didn't implement their protocols properly. What am I trying to say? Know the student handbook guidelines and how they operate to ensure that it's being appropriately executed for your children. Don't just accept what is given by the school for your children. Be that empowered parent!

If you are new to the world of the school system, here are a few questions to consider or ask about the student handbook:

Student Attendance & Makeup Work

- If my child has consecutive excused absences, how long does he/she have to complete the missing work?

- Is there a teacher or staff member who can assist my child, if he/she doesn't understand the makeup work that was provided by the teacher?

Student Discipline

- How does the teacher's classroom rules and consequences align with the school's code of conduct in the student handbook?

- When an infraction is assigned, what were the identified factors/behaviors in the school's decision?

- Were interventions, such as counseling, lunch detention, in-school suspension, or peer mediation, available? If so, was it used? If not, please explain.

- Based on the student handbook, which level/tier was used to implement the infraction because the same behavior may be listed in several levels/tiers? Was the incident aligned to the frequency of the displayed behavior?

If I had a dollar for every parent who asked this next question, I'd be a millionaire. When your child receives a consequence for an infraction, the burning question is, what happened to the other student? Did they receive the same consequence? Most times the motivation for the question is to ensure fairness for your child.

However, the Privacy laws hinder the school employees' ability to discuss student information unless you are the parent/guardian. Although you may not like the protocol, you will have to trust that the school leader exercised fair and just practices as it pertains to student discipline.

Technology Use

- What are the school district's student technology use protocols, specifically for my child's grade/school?
- As it relates to my child's cell phone usage, are the technology protocols being implemented in every classroom?

- If some teachers are enforcing the technology protocol and others are allowing students to use their cell phone, what message does this send to my children?

- It is fair to assign a consequence to students who don't comply with school protocols when there are mixed messages from the adults in the building?

Chapter 6: Your Powers

On a battlefield, war is the direct result of a conflict. This quarrel has somehow evolved due to two opposing convictions. In the middle of these two views lays the unseen influence of power. The desire for control and dominance has impacted how we live our lives in society. It appears that everyone wants to have a piece of the power pie. Like the wind, the only evidence that it exists is because of its turbulent and unpredictable forces. Although an invisible energy, its destruction can be seen in the history books due to its massive overturn of nations. If you are lucky enough to taste its sweet rewards and fail to manage its intensity, similar to a drug addict, its uncontrollable impulses may lead you off course. As a parent, whether you know it or not, you will experience an opposing belief or opinion in the school system and you need to identify your power source to win the battle.

What's interesting about power is that all of us have it. We possess the will power to not eat that last piece of cake because we want to live a healthier lifestyle. As a wife/husband, you may persuade your spouse to attend an event that is appears boring but exciting to you. As an area expert on your job, your supervisor may need you to make a decision for your company. Regardless of the types or levels of power that exist, its motivation lurks deep inside our hearts. The ultimate goal is to not let it get the best of you!

In earlier chapters, you learned about the landscape of a school district. In addition, we discussed the roles and responsibilities of its players and the resources that they use to work in the ecosystem. As I outlined the playbook strategies that you will need to leverage the school system, all of my mother's words of wisdom filled the page. Although it's been seven years since her passing, every day I hear her voice in my head as I methodically create plans and execute my actions. The need to use the art of war in schools principles are key because it requires our discernment and perception. Many times, it is the direct result of generations of people who have experienced life's challenges and learned lessons along the way. If we take the time to glean from its knowledge, its seeds will produce success in our endeavors.

In honor of my mother, the late Louise K. Elliott, and all of the mothers before her, I'm going to coin these insightful nuggets of wisdom as "My Momma Said....". While at first the sayings may sound funny or trigger childhood memories, however; momma was right about many things. Although she wasn't a military general, like Sun Tzu, her wise words could win any war that dared to cross her path.

1. My momma said to know your people and know your kind.

In the classroom, teachers use a social association chart for classroom management. The chart is a replica of the classroom furniture such as the students' desks and chairs but drawn on paper. On the first day of school as each student is assigned to his/her seat, the teacher writes the student's names on her classroom replica paper in an effort to remember the seating arrangement of students. Over the next few days of school as the teacher moves around the classroom, she observes the positive and negative interactions among students. In an effort to keep track of the student interactions, the teacher draws a connecting line from the assigned student desk to other assigned student desk on her replica classroom paper to denote interaction between the students. After the first week of school, the teacher reviews the notations of the students who have demonstrated an increase in their social interactions. In essence, the teacher is able to identify the social butterflies, also known as talkers, because there is a connecting line from that student's desk to all of the other students' desks around him/her. In addition, the teacher is also able to identify that some students will join the talkative student in conversation, while others will simply ignore him/her. As a result, this information is used to rearrange the seating assignments of students in the classroom, which minimizes disruptions.

As a parent, you need to know the social association of the players in the school district's ecosystem. Although you will not draw a geographical map replica of your community, you definitely want to take notes of the interconnectedness (negative/positive) of the players. Knowledge of this information will help you when it's time to consider your angles and options to create a plan and implement your strategies.

The following questions will help you to easily identify the social associations:

- Which players are married, relatives or friends?

- Which players are members of the same organization (church, fraternity/sorority, civic group, team sports, etc.)?

- Which players live or grew up in the same area (subdivision, neighborhood, town)?

- Which players have worked or currently working with each other?

- Which players are high school or college alumni?

After reading these questions, you may have an array of other questions to consider in this process. Others of you may be thinking that I have gone overboard because finding out these answers will take too long. You may even wonder if I have lost it or questioned if someone dropped me on my head as a baby. Trust me, these answers matter! No, you don't have to be Inspector Gadget or hire a private investigator. Therefore, let me explain why you need to know this information. Then I'll tell you how to gather your intel.

If the players know each other, this increases their chances of receiving favorable outcomes. Let's think about it. Don't you look out for people that you know? It's all psychological and natural. Due to the wiring in our brains, we tend to look out for those in our "circle". Heck, we look out for people that's not even in our circle but we are familiar with them because it's better to root for someone that you know than the unknown. As a result of a favor, loyalty is increased among the players, which strengthens their bond in the ecosystem.

Again, you are probably saying that this is too much work! I just wanted my children to attend a great school and receive a quality education. Well, guess what? This information will help you to better leverage your targets and actions. Discovery of this information is actually very easy because it only requires your eyes. So breathe. In fact, as you are reading this book, the faces and interactions of some players have already come to your mind. You most likely didn't know its significance but now you know its name because social associations matter.

One way to learn the interconnectedness of the players is to be observant when you attend community events, such as a school board meeting, county commissioner meeting, or high school football game. Although this may sound funny, attending holiday parties will yield great intel because people become more relaxed with music and a little alcohol. It’s something about that truth serum that allows you to really know what’s on a person’s mind.

As you become aware of your surroundings, take note of those who are interacting before, during and after the event. Also, take note of those who give friendly nods and smiles to each other across the room, especially when certain comments are made by the attendees. As you get into your vehicle to go home, pay attention to the parking lot meetings. Yes, the parking lot meetings can be very interesting. Sometimes parking lot meetings occur because the players are discussing private and important information and they don't want anyone to hear them. Although all of your answers won't be evidenced after one meeting, each time, you will see more social associations because your awareness has been activated to notice it.

It's similar to your vehicle. You may have driven by a certain make/model car for years. However, as soon as you purchase that vehicle, you somehow are able to notice that your vehicle is everywhere. The crazy part is that the vehicle has always been there. Dealers produce thousands of the same vehicle each year. However, your awareness of the vehicle became alive once experienced it.

Similarly, knowledge of your school district ecosystem's social associations will become visibly evident because of your cognitive brain function. This information will assist you in your planning phase, if you ever have a problem in the school system. All great warriors recognize that you must know yourself and your enemies. Please note that everyone in your school district community is not your enemy, so you definitely need to identify and become acquainted with their allies. If there is an issue, you need to know who will stand by your side to help you or have selective anemia. In addition, this will assist you, if you need intel to make a decision. The last thing that you need is for the opposing view to have knowledge of your information and angle because like you, they will use it to their advantage.

For example, the school district is seeking to implement a curriculum that you philosophically oppose. In order to increase awareness and support, you need to get the word out. Would you go the people who live a lifestyle contrary to yours and in support of the new curriculum? No, you would go to people who share similar values. Would you seek advocates from those who are on the fence? Well, it depends on who they are connected to in the landscape, as well as their allegiance. You don't need any flip floppers around you or people who play both sides. The decisions in this process are not precise, but art, which requires your unique creative power and skill. Overall, access to the social associations in your ecosystem is crucial. As my momma said, you need to know your people and know your kind.

2. My momma said don’t let your left hand know what your right hand knows.

Just because you have access to information doesn't mean that you have to let it be known to others. When interacting with the players in the ecosystem, use discretion. They don't need to know what you know or who you know. If you acquire information that's hard to access about the school district or have a relationship with a major power player in the school system, keep it to yourself. That information could be useful in the future so store it in your long-term memory box. You never know when you will need to go another route.

I recall a situation with a parent who had been experiencing problems at her child’s school. It appeared as though no one cared about the plight of her son. Her emails fell on deaf ears. A couple of the teachers, who were included in the emails, noticed that certain staff members weren’t being responsive to the parent. In an effort to assist the parent, the teachers reached out to the other staff members to try to intervene on the parent's behalf. When the teachers approached the staff members about their apparent lack of care or concern, the responsive staff members became angry because the nonresponsive staff members shared "how they really felt". Their response wasn't aimed at the parent or her son, but rather them being disgruntled employees, who had become disengaged at work.

As a result, when the parent spoke to the responsive teachers, they "armed" the parent with detailed information. The parent was able to use the information to get assistance for her child from central office leaders. Although the central office staff didn't know the source of the information, the parent was able to strategize to receive the attention and support that she needed to ensure academic success for her child. Overall, it wasn't about being a talebearer to school leadership, although the parent would have been well within her rights. Her time and energy were focused was on her child. In the end, the parent was able to better advocate for her child because of the access to information. Like my momma said, don't let your left hand know what your right hand knows.

3. My momma said that a wise man keeps a still tongue.

Honestly speaking, this golden nugget was a challenge and it took me a little time to implement with proficiency. Somehow, I always felt that if I didn't speak what was on my mind, people would take advantage of me or see me as being weak. If you are one of those people, who must tell someone off or you need to get the record straight, you definitely need my momma's nugget.

As a parent, you can't "go off" on people, even if you believe that you are right. It's all about the timing, words, and impact of your behavior. Surprisingly, it's not about whether the information was right or wrong but simply was it the right time? In addition, if those words come out of your mouth, what will happen next? I'm not just talking about the next minute but the next day or the next week or the next month. Will your words be a catalyst to set off a fire storm that you won't be able to contain? Sometimes you have to appear weak when you are actually strong. You have to be able to read the room and know when to remain silent. I know that it may be hard for you but zip it!

This wise tip is also helpful if you are one of those parents who is "overly vocal" at school. Just in case you are wondering if it's you, answer one question: Have you ever been threatened to be banned from school property? If you replied yes, then you might be that parent. Here's another one, after speaking to an employee at your child's school, has your child looked embarrassed afterwards, then you might be that parent. If your voice can be heard down the hallway and you don't have a bullhorn, then you might be that parent. If you hear that your child is heard saying, "Don't let me have my momma come up here", then you might be that parent. If you have ever threatened to contact your lawyer on the school or thought about calling your lawyer on "those people" at that school, then you might be that parent.

Please understand that we are all human and at times say things that we may later regret. However, if you raise your voice or use inappropriate words towards school employees, you are turning them off. Simply put, they may not like you and will probably try to avoid you. Now, if are still "that parent", you are probably thinking that you don't care if they don't like you. In fact, you don't pay people to like you because you already have friends. While all of this may be true, staff avoidance of you may also lead to you not getting the help that you need to support your children because they don't want to be bothered with you and your drama. Yes, I said it and I know that you are probably surprised by that statement. Again, I'm trying to help you win so you need to know the impact of your actions, if you are one of "those parents".

Although school employees are professionals, they are still human and have feelings. Avoiding the explosive encounters simply means that people don't always have to know everything that you are thinking. It also means that when you are talking, pay attention to your tone, volume, and body language. That's why we have one mouth and two ears. We should listen twice as much as we speak. While you may be thinking, how is that a strategy to help me leverage the school system? My response to you is that it's hard to acquire a target in a school system if you don't have any players to play with. You'll catch more flies with honey than with vinegar! As my momma said, a wise man keeps a still tongue.

4. My momma said to walk softly but carry a big stick.

As a child this phrase sounded strange because what did a big stick have anything to do with how I walked? I soon learned that it was an analogy. She was teaching me to be kind and gentle towards others even if I was in control. When we walk softly, we have a desire to do good and be considerate of others. Having a big stick means that I have some form of power or authority that I could easily use but I choose not to. Although you may have influence, act unassuming.

In a war, there are direct and indirect hits in the battle that lead to victory. Although, you may have the upper hand in a situation, that doesn't mean that you have to be boastful. Be the quiet storm. Quiet storms are those people who are calm. They may not say a lot but when they speak, everyone stops to listen because the information is meaningful. Quiet storms are reserved. They are self-aware and don't have anything to prove to anyone. Finally, quiet storms are observant and reflective. However, with just one swift move you could be destroyed because they are power-packed and will show up out of nowhere.

As a parent, there's no need to lead with your title. I understand that you want to command respect and you may think that using your title will get the school's attention. As for me, I purposely don't include my title when I speak to school staff. First, I want to know how they treat all parents, regardless of status. If school staff respond to me in a timely manner, I love it because they are more likely to respond to all parents in the same manner. As a person who loves great customer service, their response lets me know the type of people that I am working with in the building. Although I don't know them personally, their response gives me a small peek into their character and work ethic.

On the contrary, on rare occasions, if the staff employee is very unprofessional or repeatedly unresponsive to you, then showing your "big stick" is most definitely appropriate. Sometimes people need to be reminded that they don't know who they are engaging and they must treat everyone fairly. These instances are called a reality check and it's purpose is meant to redirect inappropriate behaviors. That doesn't mean that you should use dynamite but a lighter may do the trick. As my momma said, walk softly but carry a big stick.

5. My momma said to not throw the baby out with the bathwater.

Although there may be some negative things that you don't like about your school, that doesn't mean that you should get rid of the whole school. Your children's school is valuable and it is necessary for your children to learn. As a parent, you have to figure out how to strategically remove or weed out the school's weaknesses, while keeping its strengths. You must be reflective and be deliberate in your actions.

Just in case you didn't know this information, all school districts know that there are problems in their system. They also know that you know what they know about the school district. It's not a secret. The only difference between the school district and you, is how you arrived at your conclusion. The school district has data to support their concerns. While you have "word on the street" as your evidence. It really doesn't matter who is right, wrong, or indifferent. In these cases, both sides must disarm themselves and join forces because you are stronger together.

Although I spoke about the Strategic plan in the resources section, I am going to expand on it because of its importance. This plan is a five-year plan that outlines the school district's goals, objectives and tasks. As a parent you can help steer the direction of the school district's strategic plan by

1. Completing the survey requests when it's emailed to you.
2. Attend the district's call to action meetings.
3. Consistently participate in your child's school parent advisory council.

School districts are always seeking your thoughts for ways to improve. Unfortunately, what usually happens is that there is no representation from all demographics (such as grade levels, region, race, and economic status), as well as student subgroups (such as students with disabilities, limited English proficiency, and economically disadvantaged). When there is no representation for your group, other parents make decisions for you and your children. Although those parents have the best of intentions, they may not know your struggles or needs. As a result, the school district's decision may be ineffective for you but effective for them. With your participation, the school is able to be inclusive of everyone because there is not a one size fits all for educating students.

If you are a working class parent, I understand that you have to work to pay your bills. I know that if you take off from work, you don' get paid because your company doesn't have leave benefits. However, if you aren't able to be present in a meeting, contact the school to see the other options. Perhaps the meeting could be available by conference call, Facebook Live, Zoom, or recorded. Also, you could request a copy of the meeting notes and provide your feedback to the meeting facilitator by email. Although you may be physically absent that doesn't mean that you can't be actively engaged in your children's school. Where there is a will, there is a way!

The following story is an example of how our system strategized to be inclusive of all parents. Each quarter our schools held parent teacher conferences to discuss students' report cards. Our schools scheduled these meetings during the school day. Based on parent feedback, the meeting hours were held from 8:00am to 4:00pm. However, we noticed that there was a group of parents who did not attend the meeting. In an effort to increase parental engagement, we took great strides to contact them to ask why they missed the meeting and what could be done to ensure their participation. Once parents informed us of their work schedule conflict, we modified the hours to meet their needs. We revamped the conferences by extending the meeting time from 11:00am to 7:00pm on day one and 8:00am to 12:00pm the next day. As a result, we were able to drastically increase the parent participation rate.

Overall, there will always be something to resolve in your child's school system because we are imperfect people. Sometimes school systems get it right and you are happy. Then there are those times when the district for whatever reason crashes and burns. Although you will not be pleased by the debris and smell of smoke, that doesn't equate to your school being deemed as a failure. Like the phoenix, your school system has the capacity to rise through the ashes because as a community working together, you are stronger and powerful. Like my momma said, don't throw the baby out with the bathwater.

6. My momma said waste not want not.

In the midst of the pandemic and students returning to schools, it has been filled with great angst. As a parent, I understand because I didn't want my son to contract the Coronavirus. While his school system put measures in place to deter the spread, I still felt uneasy because of my compromised immune system. In the end, my son was very careful at school and adhered to all of the rules to keep it at bay.

What's interesting is that for over 100 years, the United States of America has always been in a constant state of health crisis. Unfortunately, these infectious diseases have resulted in the illness and death millions of people. If it wasn't the Spanish flu, it was the Asian flu. If it wasn't the swine flu, it was the HIV/AIDS pandemic. If the Coronavirus wasn't enough, we now have the monkey pox. We live in a world of persistent turmoil. With the presence of each pandemic, it somehow leads our economy into a recession and limits our funding sources.

As a parent, you have most likely felt the impact financially as well. It seems like the food and gas prices have doubled. Yet, our paychecks have remained the same. To top if off, our children still have academic needs that must be addressed because of the impact of virtual learning. Although many schools have implemented remediation plans, your children may still require additional support. In these times they may require tutoring. However, you don't have the means due to the cost. Don't become despaired because your personal educational advocate is here to help you! I am going to show you how you can get the same information from your child's school for free. Yes, free! Well, it's not exactly free because our tax dollars paid for it but you get the point.

You may or may not know but teachers have tons of resources. The school's bookroom and teacher classroom closets are filled to capacity with instructional materials. They are busting at the seams with years and years of stuff, especially if they have been teaching for a long time. In addition, schools have purchased a wealth of online educational programs. Between the resources provided by the state and school, there aren't enough hours in the school day to teach all of that information.

Your child's teacher is one of your greatest assets because he/she knows your child's specific academic needs. They have access to the internal and state assessment results. In addition, your school has customized tutorial applications that are tailor-made for your children that can be accessed on the internet. All great warriors know that if an opportunity is to your advantage, use it. Securing these prescriptive materials for your children is definitely beneficial.

In order to preserve your money, the following are several items that you can do to continue your children's learning:

- Create a quiet space for your children to read daily for at least 20 minutes. Studies show a correlation between the frequency of reading and the time spent reading. If your children are not reading on grade level, establish a consistent time to read each day. If your children are on or above grade level, reading ensures that they don't slide back to a lower level. This is especially crucial over the summertime. Yes, it's their vacation time but setting aside 20 minutes within a 24-hour time period will not kill them. Celebrate reading with your children to increase their motivation. Once they fall in love with reading, you will see them soar academically. You'll be surprised at the amount of growth from just 20 minutes!

- When you and your children are in the car, play games with the items in your environment. For example, read the street and store signs. See how many vehicle tags they can remember at a time. Count the number of passing vehicles. Give them the map to read to provide the directions. Take a walk in the park and talk about the kinds of flowers, trees, or animals that they see. Everywhere you go can become a mobile classroom because learning is all around us!

- At the end of the school year, see if your children's teacher has any books, workbooks or materials that they are looking to discard. As schools purchase new textbooks, they have no use for the previous collection. Sometimes school districts are able to sell old textbooks back to the publishing companies for a small profit. Other times, schools throw those books away. You never know unless you ask.

Take advantage of the free available resources. Like my momma said, waste not want not.

7. My momma said rolling stones don't gather no moss.

When I was a college student living off campus, I moved around a lot. My goal was to find the cheapest housing in order to save money. One day when my parents came to visit me, they discovered that my house number had been changed again. During that time, I didn't have a cell phone so each time I moved, the home number changed. As my mother's frustration began to rise because of the constant changes and her desire to remember which one was my newest number on her notepad, she gave me this nugget.

It's impossible for rolling stones to gather moss with constant movement. An interesting point about growing moss on rocks is that in the proper temperature, it's easy to maintain. This concept also applies to a consistent education for students in school. There may a time in your life when you may find yourself unemployed and homeless. Although there may be changes all around you and your children, school is the one place that can provide stability and comfort for your children.

Similar to the moss, it's much easier to maintain your children's education when they are able to stay in the same school. There are federally funded programs, like the McKinney-Vento Act, to ensure that your children's education is not impacted by your financial crisis. This program provides a range of benefits to support you. One of those items include allowing your children to remain in their school, regardless of your current residence. In addition, the school district receives funds to provide free transportation for your children to get to school. If a district school bus doesn't serve your area of temporary residence due to zoning, the district will assign an employee to transport your children to and from school.

Rolling stones don't gather any moss when there is a high employee turnover in your school district. If there is a new school Superintendent, principal or teacher every other year, you should be very concerned. This constant change impacts the academic achievement for students. Simply put, experienced teachers and institutional knowledge impact students' success. Although new teachers are qualified and eager to teach, everything in the school district and school is still new to them. They may need additional time to learn their new landscape and the rules of the school district ecosystem. In addition, employee turnover disrupts the collegial culture because quality relationships take time to build.

A high employee turnover in a school district also impacts the district's budget. According to the Learning Policy Institute, it costs between $9,000 to $21,000 in resources and personnel time to recruit and train each new teacher. Yes, each new teacher. For example, if a school district were to lose 100 teachers each year, they are diverting millions of dollars from the school district's budget. I dare say, it costs even more money to recruit school leadership. Just think, this is money that could be used to teach your children and improve their school.

Now you may be wondering what's going on in my children's school district. First, we live in a day and time, where people will resign from a job at the drop of a hat. However, this is not always the case for school district employees. If you were to poll district employees, you would discover that most of them don't leave for a higher paycheck. Many leave because of the increasing mandates and staff morale. Whatever the reason for their departure, something must be done to stop the bleeding. As a parent, you have a voice on the matter. Some of the options include contacting your school district to find out why employees are leaving and what can be done to rectify the issues. No, you or they may not have all of the answers but it starts with a willingness to partner with your school district to start the conversation. Just as your children need to be in a consistent school environment to learn, your children's teachers must be there in order to provide instruction. Like my momma said rolling stones don't gather no moss.

8. My momma said keep your eyes and wits about you.

Growing up in rural South Carolina, my family listened to various genres of music. In my days, we had a record player and an eight track. You are probably wondering my age right now. Don't worry because we later transitioned to more advanced technology. In middle and high school, we had cassette players and CD discs. Anyway, there was always a message or theme to the song's lyrics that we could apply in our life. It was like the singers knew us and were speaking directly to us about our circumstances.

On this particular day, Kenny Roger's husky, baritone voice filled the air. Having heard the song numerous times, everyone in the room started singing the words. "You've got to know when to hold 'em. Know when to fold 'em. Know when to walk away. And know when to run." Yes, the song is called The Gambler. What's interesting about the application of the song was that although he was talking about his gambling strategies, metaphorically, he was also taking about life.

Everything isn't for everybody. Just because you saw it done in another state or school district doesn't mean that it will work in your school district. Yes, the company's sale representatives are going to say that it works for all students. However, that may not the case. For example, every clothing store dress doesn't look good on everybody. Yes, it's available for everyone to purchase. However, depending on the person's body shape and dimensions, it will look very different.

I know that you want to solve every issue that you may have with your school district. However, there will be times when you may have to "hold" or "fold". Yes, holding means that you are going to keep pressing the issue because you know that you will get results. Then there are times when you will have to stop or withdraw yourself from the situation because staying will make things worse. Knowing the difference requires strategy! All warriors know that you've got to be aware of the capacity of your landscape and players when making decisions. In addition, you may have to identify unexpected routes to reach your goals. As you are moving and shaking, don't allow your ego to affect the final outcome because we all have blind spots. Keep your eyes open but also use your brain. My momma said, keep your eyes and wits about you.

9. My momma said actions speak louder than words.

It doesn’t matter who you are, where you grew up, your race, religion, or creed, we have all experienced someone in our life who has said one thing and done the opposite. When the happens, we may feel betrayed and hurt. Sometimes I wonder if the person had a character flaw. Why would you tell me to trust you then stab me in the back? Do you know the definition of a friend? Is this how you want to be treated? What would make you want to act contrary to your words?

While we may never get the real answers, identical scenarios play out more frequently than we’d probably like to admit. Based on the frequency of betrayal, you may have developed trust issues with people. I’m not here to judge. However, those feelings aren’t isolated to just relationships because they play out in every area of our life.

Unfortunately, similar to every occupation, there may be times when a district employee may not shed a great light on the organization, leaving you with a bad impression of the school district. They may have promised you something and later had defaulted on it. My hope is that this never happens to you. However, if you have made several attempts to resolve the issue, stop talking about it. It's now time to write about it! Write about it because your actions have to speak louder than your words.

The following strategies will assist you in resolving your problems in your children's school. This method is my secret to being labeled, "Document Queen" because I have a very high success rate in achieving my goals due to my copious note taking skills. Implementing this game plan will send a clear message that you are serious and it will command respect.

- Documentation Matters

- Secure a journal, notebook, or computer program to record your contacts with the school.
- During each conversation with the staff employee (in-person or phone call), write down the date/time, attendees, and the main points discussed during the meeting.
- If the communication is by email, you may either draft a note in your journal, notebook, or move the email correspondence to a folder labeled school communication.
- Organization is very important when you are documenting because you have to remember where you placed your materials. In addition, you want to be able to easily assess your information.
- Your children don't need to know the location of your journal. This comment is not meant to question your parenting skills. However, children love to snoop so keep this information locked up in a safe place.

- Follow-Through Matters

- After each meeting/conversation, send the attendees a quick email:
    - Statement #1 - Thank them for taking the time to meet or speak with you on the identified date.
    - Statement #2 – State the purpose for the meeting
    - Statement # 3 - State the agreed upon resolution
    - Statement #4 – State the next steps
- The correspondence should be clear and succinct. No long essays. Just four sentences.
- This will only take you no more than five minutes to write. If it's longer than five minutes, you are typing too much information.

- Chain of Command Matters
    - Identify your school district's organizational chart. This can be found on the district website. Google "organizational chart and the school year" (organizational chart 2022). Note: The school district's

organizational doesn't include school staff, only central office.

- Example chain of command for most school districts:
  - Teacher
  - Assistant principal
  - Principal
  - Principal supervisor
  - Supervisor's supervisor
  - Superintendent
  - Board of Education
- Follow your school district's chain of command, if you have any issues.
- Start your communication with only the conflicting person. In your initial email, do not cc' others. Keep the matter between the involved parties.
- If you email the teacher/staff member and 1. The problem persists or 2. The problem is unresolved, you may email the next level person (employee's supervisor), such as the assistant principal or principal.
- As you progress up the chain of command, don't rewrite a new email to the staff member with your concerns. Locate and forward the

original email with the conflicting employee. In your correspondence, inform the staff employee that this matter has not been resolved and you are seeking a resolution.

- Statement # 1 – Thank you for taking the time to review my concerns.
- Statement # 2 – In an attempt to resolve the matter, please review the email correspondence below.

A Word to the Wise

Following the school district's chain of command is essential in maintaining order. Noncompliance, may be perceived as someone who doesn't understand the organization's structure or someone who doesn't care about following the rules because you are above them. Also, if you don't follow the chain of command, most times you will be redirected. For example, if you skipped over the teacher and contacted the principal, he/she will direct you to the teacher. If you skip over everyone and contact the Board of Education, they will redirect you to the school Superintendent, who is the Board of Education's point person. The school Superintendent will reroute you to the proper person.

Please don't jump the established school district's chain of command. Although you may know the principal, that doesn't mean that you should direct your concerns there. If a board member is your relative or friend, don't try to use that relationship for your benefit, especially when it comes to the chain of command in the school district. When you don't follow the chain of command, other staff members will find out because nothing is ever a secret. Someone will know what happened because people talk. Also, the board member's actions may shed a bad light on their character and work-ethic. This behavior will infest, spread, and destroy the school district's culture. Then everyone will want to seek favors from their people because they believe that if the rules didn't matter to the governing body of the organization, why should it matter to them.

This is not the wild, wild west. School districts have systems and structures for a reason. It ensures equitable practices for everyone. When you have an issue in your children's school district, please follow the established protocols. Using the outlined steps listed above will guarantee you success every time because documentation matters, follow-through matters, and the chain of command matters. Like my momma said, actions speak louder than words.

10. My momma said, two wrongs don't make a right.

The United States of America established the Bill of Rights in the Constitution to establish our liberties as citizens. What's interesting is that aside from our history lessons in school, many of us don't know most of them. We usually speak of our freedom of speech and the right to bear arms. However, are we aware of the other eight amendments? Usually, it's only when we believe that we have been violated that we seek assistance from legal services to confirm the existence of the other eight amendments.

This limited knowledge of rights is probably the same when it comes to your parental and children's rights in the school district. Are you aware of your rights in the district's ecosystem? Do you know where the rights are located? Do you review your rights before or after you have a problem at your child's school? What's interesting is that your rights outlines the guaranteed power that has been freely given on the landscape, yet very few parents or students take the time to understand or implement it. On the battlefield if a warrior doesn't know the location of his/her weapons or how to use it, when the enemy approaches, he will be slaughtered. The strong, mighty soldier's demise was a result of his inability to recognize his power.

The fact that you are reading this book tells me that are a fearless, tenacious frontrunner. Once you become equipped with understanding your parental and student rights, you will be a force to be reckoned with in the landscape! Your ability to advocate and support your children will be through the roof when coupled with the strategies in this playbook. When I think about you being an empowered parent who reproduces other parents, this will become a movement.

You may be wondering who are the two wrong people and why is it not right? As a parent, when you don't have access to the correct information, you tend to make mistakes. On the other hand, if the staff employee is aware of your confusion or misguided information, which may or may not be in the best interest of your children, that is incorrect. Although both parties are wrong that doesn't make the situation right.

I've been in the educational field for almost 30 years and I've witnessed a lot. I recall a time when a special education student was displaying very inappropriate behavior in class. As a result, the administrator contacted his mother to inform her of his actions. Prior to calling the mother, the administrator reviewed the student's discipline records and determined that suspending the student would trigger a host of other actions due to the federal law guidelines. Rather than suspend the student, she elected to provide the student "a pass". The administrator convinced the parent that another suspension would be viewed as a negative for her child. In an effort to help him, she would allow the student to come home to "cool off".

As a parent, who didn't want a negative report on her son's record, she was eager to come pick her son from school. However, the parent wasn't aware that the school employee's actions were not legal. When I think about this story, some 20 years later, it still saddens me because I hate for people to be taken advantage of in any situation. My only hope is that this was a rare occurrence and staff employees are adhering to the federal laws for students with disabilities, despite parents' limited knowledge.

Now you may be wondering, what are some things that I should be looking out for? Well, I'm glad that you asked because I'm going to give you a few areas to keep on your radar in your ecosystem.

1. Parent & Student Rights
   In the resources chapter, I mentioned the Board of Education's policies. The school district will provide in detail those rights. Although it defers by school district, the nonnegotiables speak of items such as, the right to provide a free education, the right to not be discriminated against, and the right to be safe in school.

   The following questions/tips may aide you:

a. You have a right to know if your child's teacher is certified. If this is the case, you want to ask the school what types of support will the teacher be receiving to ensure your child isn't impacted adversely? What will be the course of action if your child doesn't do well in the class? If your child is not progressing in the class, is transferring to a certified teacher's class an option?
b. What if the school district curriculum addresses a subject that is against your philosophical views, such as creationism or sex education? Notify the school immediately, inform them of your concern, and request for an alternative assignment.

On the other hand, your next statement may be that you don't know what is covered in the curriculum to ask that question. If that is the case, reach out to the Director of Curriculum in central office. Inform them of your concern and ask if there are any conflicting concepts in your child's grade. Once you know, make the request for an alternative assignment.

Another item that you must know about is that many school districts will send an "opt out" letter for you to sign, if they are teaching information that may be an issue to you. If you don't sign, it means automatic consent and your children will be included in the lesson.

c. Can any employee access my child's personal information, such as grades, health record, discipline, tests, etc.? Depending upon the level of access certain employees have access to student records. However, to ensure that the rights of students are protected, employees may only access the student's records, if it is aligned to their job duty, and it is necessary to complete a task for work. In order to protect the students, there is a policy outlined by the Board of Education. Noncompliance of any policy by an employee will result in punitive actions. For example, a student's assigned teacher may review the grades and test scores from the previous school years to support the student academically. However, if the school secretary heard that you moved into an expensive home and out of curiosity, she reviews your child's records, this is a violation.

The Privacy Act also protects the rights of your child as it pertains to guardianship. When a student is enrolled in school, certain documents are required to provide evidence of your parental rights. If another adult, contacts or visits the school to request information on your children, the request will be denied by the staff employee. In addition, this also applies to birth parents, who have lost their guardianship rights. For example, if the student's guardian is a foster care parent, although you are the child's birth parent, you will not receive access or information on your children.

2. Student Grades

   Based on the school district, there are an array of grading practices. One district may say that an A letter-grade is equivalent to 90% - 100%, while another school district may say that an A letter-grade is equivalent to 93% - 100%. You may ask, why? The answer lies between the Superintendent and Board of Education. If you would like additional information on the rationale, contact the Office of Curriculum and Instruction.

   The following are questions that you may consider concerning your child's grades:

   a. How many grades are required each quarter for my child's grades? At the end of the quarter, did my child's teacher into the minimum required grades in the school portal?

   b. How did the district decide on the assignment (such as homework, classwork, test/quiz, and projects) percentages? The purpose for this question is due to the sometimes high test/quiz percentages and the low homework/class percentages. For example, if a teacher is required to submit two tests per quarter and tests are 50%, that means that each test was 25% of your child's grade.

c. When I check the school's online portal for my child's grades, I noticed that the grades are usually uploaded at the middle and end of the quarter. What should I do? Teachers are required to enter grades in the school's portal minimally on a biweekly basis. After two weeks, if you notice that there are no posted grades, start the documentation process by contacting the teacher. Generally speaking, it is unfair to expect you to support your child academically, if you don't know his/her grades. If you notice a pattern of missing grades, contact the principal.

d. If my child is failing a class this quarter and I was never notified by the school, what should I do? The school is required to inform you, if your child is in danger of failing or failing a class. If your child is failing a class, you should receive formal notification in writing. Failure to inform you could result in an array of options, such as giving your child additional time to complete the work, alternative projects, or a passing grade due to the school's negligence to notify you. If you foresee this as a concern, start your documentation protocol.

3. If your child has an Individualized Education Plan (IEP), the federal government laws protect the educational rights of children with disabilities. In addition, review the special education parent rights and responsibilities manual to ensure that your child is receiving an appropriate education.

   The following are questions to consider:

   a. Is my child receiving the services and/or service hours outlined in the IEP? If the answer is no, request a meeting to implement a plan of action. Some options may include increasing contact time during the school year and/or assigning the student to Extended School Year (ESY), which is held in the summer.

b. If your child refuses to receive services, there may be times that the school isn't held liable. It depends on the situation. Request that the school inform you immediately, if your child refuses services. There may be a reason and everyone (parent and school staff) need to know why so that it can be resolved as soon as possible.

c. Can my child be suspended? Yes, the school is required to follow the code of conduct. However, a manifestation meeting may alter the results due to the student's disability.

d. What if you don't know how to support your child in school? You have several people to contact:

    i. School special education teacher or coordinator
    ii. Special Education office
    iii. Parent Engagement office

Don't feel embarrassed. They are there to support you.

e. My child has an IEP for one disability but there appears to be another problem. What can I do? Request in writing to have an IEP meeting. At the meeting request for additional testing. Ask for the testing and results timeline. Do not accept the option of waiting until the next school year. Time is of the essence.
f. What if I have concerns about my child but he/she does not have an IEP and I want him/her to tested? Email your child's teacher and principal to share your concerns and to request testing. Your child's school is required to complete this process within a set timeframe. Generally speaking, within about 90-120 days, you should have a response of the status. If this doesn't happen, forward

your original email request to the central office, Special education director.

Like my, momma said two wrongs don't make a right.

11. My momma said, if it had been a snake, it would have bitten you.

I vividly recall my mother cooking dinner for our family. In an effort to assist her, she instructed me to retrieve a can out of the pantry. As I looked for the requested item on the shelf, I couldn't find it and informed her that it was not there. In an effort to assist me, my mother told me to look on the second shelf for the can. Once more I looked in the pantry and I was not able to locate it. As a result of my inability to find the can, my mother walked over to the pantry to join me. Leaning into the pantry, she pointed to the can on the second shelf, which was behind a box of cereal. As my mother walked back over to the stove to finish cooking, she shook her head and said that if it was a snake, it would have bitten me. With a confused face from her statement, she replied that the can was right in front of my face and all I had to do was look for it.

All great warriors know that they must always be alert. At any time, you may be summoned to protect and defend yourself. Like Spider man, you have to always keep one ear open to ensure that everyone is safe. Somehow he knew that the tingling sensors in his body detected danger and he was off to save the day.

As a parent, you have that innate Spidey-sense to protect your children. Although there is no visible evidence, your sensors somehow perceive pending danger. If something feels wrong in reference to your children, investigate it. If something looks off, ask questions. You know your child's personality so if they come home sad or disoriented, take the time to explore the root cause. If your child cries when its time to go to school and he/she is normally excited about school, explore the reason for the sudden change in behavior. Although some people may call you a "mother hen" or "father bear", it's better to be labeled an overprotective parent, than allow your child to be hurt or abused. Please don't minimize bullying because it will have an impact on your children. If you suspect trouble, start looking for the snake. Like my momma said, if it had been a snake, it would have bitten you.

12. My momma said strike when the iron is hot.

As a result of the Coronavirus, families have been robbing from Peter to pay Paul. Millions of people lost their jobs and were forced to enroll in government assistance programs in order to provide for their families. With limited income coming in your household, now the school is sending home an exhaustive school supply list for your children. From agenda notebooks to gym uniforms to book fees to locker fees, you may start to feel overwhelmed from it all. Before you throw in the towel, please know that there is a solution.

Based on your income, you may possibly qualify under the Title I program at your child's school. The federal government annually distributes additional money to school districts based on the family household income. These funds are used to ensure that all students are provided with a high-quality education.

This is the time to strike while the iron is hot! Take advantage of the opportunity. Immediately contact your school to ensure that you have completed the lunch application to identify your new status. Once this document has been processed and approved, your child will receive free breakfast and lunch for the entire school year. You don't have to worry about everyone knowing your personal business because each student is assigned a lunch number. As students retrieve their food from the cafeteria and submit their numbers to the cashier, the computer informs the student of the amount owed. Since all students have a lunch account, the source of funding is unknown.

There are many others benefits to assist you as a parent. Although school districts protocols may vary, call the Title I central office if you have any questions. The following are opportunities that may assist you:

- Field trips
  - Don't keep your children home from school because you don't have money to pay for the class field trip. When the permission slip comes home, contact the

school's counselor. Field trips are a part of Title I's "high-quality" education.

- Advanced Placement (AP) tests
  - AP classes enable your child to receive high school and college credit. There are fees associated with the exit exam. AP exams are a part of Title I's "high quality" education. Notify the counselor for additional information.

- Extended school activities
  - The school system's instructional after-school programs, tutoring, and summer school programs may all be free to you. Notify the after school coordinator or school principal.
- Parent involvement and activities
  - Transportation: Your family will receive free public transportation or taxi to and from all school related events. Notify the school secretary to inquire about the process.

- Meals: If your school plans an academic-focused meeting, they have funds to provide meals. Note: This is a very strict guideline. However, if approved, parents don't have to be worried about providing dinner for their family, if they attend an evening meeting.

The aforementioned information list is not an exhaustive list. School districts are becoming very innovative in their strategies to ensure all students have access to high-quality education. In addition, because parents are critical to a child's education, barriers are removed to ensure your engagement in the school setting. Your desire to participate in your child's education shouldn't be impacted by your financial challenges. The school has money to help you. Like my momma said, strike while the iron is hot.

13. My momma said bad news travels fast.

Do you remember the "relay a message game" in school? It was when the teacher would whisper something in the ear of the first student at the head of the line, who would have to whisper and repeat the exact words to the next person eventually making its way to the end of the line. When I was a student, we loved playing that game. It was so funny to see the awkward expressions on my classmates' faces as they listened to the incomprehensible statement and were asked to repeat it to the next student. Finally, when the student at the end of the line said what he/she had heard, the entire class would fall out laughing because it sounded like gibberish. After the teacher would state her originally sentence, the entire class had the case of the giggles because somehow it had morphed into a green-headed monster.

If you want to see a major commotion at your child's school, then hand the microphone over to the community's honorary meddling gossiper. The school's front office calls will roll in like an uncontrollably domino shuffle because parents heard very disturbing information and they must receive a response immediately because its an emergency.

Question: Why would you call your child's school because you heard that students being chased by yellow wolves and blue zebras at recess time while teachers watched and did nothing? You probably may have just reread that statement and wondered, what in the world? However, this is how bad news travels fast….and wrong!

If you happen to hear alarming information about your child's school, you should be concerned about it. However, before you pick up your matches to light up the school, reflect on the following:

- Consider the source of the information.
    - Is this the same person, who stirs up drama? Are they eager to "bring you a bone"? Did they cry wolf the last time?

- Consider what is being said
    - Does the information make sense to you? Is it credible? Based on the character of the person, is it likely to occur?
- Consider why it's being said
    - Is the action aimed to be a smear campaign? What is the purpose or motivation? If you repeat it, will it hurt or harm someone?

- Consider where it's being said
    - Is it being said in the barber or beauty shop? Enough said.

- Consider how it's being said
    - Is the person's posture different? Are they trying to lean in or whisper the information in your ear? Does the conversation start with, "Let me tell you…." or "Did you hear…" or "It's none of my business, but…."?

Did you hear the news around town? My momma said, bad news travel fast.

14. My momma said, the early bird gets the worm.

As a school leader, I still incorporate this principle in my life. Along with this phrase that my momma said, I would also hear that "to be early is to be on time and to be on time is to be late". Both of these phrases operate under the theory that your chances of success are drastically increased when you are the first to arrive because you have opportunity. You get first dibs on all accessible options. When you are able to start a project early, this puts you in a position to maximize the outcome. In essence, you are able to go farther because you took advantage of the time. As a result, you were able to seize the moment.

Due to the amount of information that I provided to you in this book, you may be a little overwhelmed because you don't know where to start. To ensure that you are able to start the school year off on the right foot, the following are actionable steps that you can start right now. This information will be instrumental to having a successful school year and allow you to take advantage of those early worms on your journey.

Calendar Alignment

Sometimes we forget things because of our busy lives. As a parent, you are juggling a lot of balls in the air at a time and you can't afford to drop any of them. However, creating a structured system to keep track of everything will ensure that you are able to better manage those never ending balls. In order to minimize the chaos in your life, aligning your children's school calendar and events with yours will aid in prioritization and scheduling. Due to the state requirements, school districts have approved the annual calendar in the spring of the previous school year. In addition, many of them have already drafted the school calendar two years in advance. Over the summer transfer the current year's calendar and events to your personal calendar. If your children are enrolled in extracurricular activities, add their schedule to the calendar as well. Also, add the PTA, School Improvement, and Board of Education meeting dates for the year.

While at first it may look like rush hour traffic on your calendar, color-coding events will add clarity because some items are actionable and others are an FYI (for your information). For example, on my calendar:

- My personal appointments and meetings are coded in black
- Birthdays and anniversaries of family and friends are coded in yellow
- Holidays are coded in green
- My children's school calendar, events, and sport activities are coded in purple

- My children's FYI events, such as report card distribution date and end of quarter dates are coded in blue.
- Share your work account calendar to your personal account calendar. This will allow you to see everything in one place on your phone.

<u>Document Binder</u>

At the beginning of the school year, you will receive about five trees worth of school documents, ranging from each teacher's contact information, class syllabus, class schedule, and school handbook. In an effort to not throw anything away, I would place the documents on my end table, which looked like a pile of trash because papers were everywhere. To make matters worse, when I needed to locate one of the teacher's email address, it was nowhere to be found. It was apparent that my system wasn't working.

In an effort to keep the documents together, create a notebook binder with pockets for each child. As each document comes home, hole-punch it and add to the binder. Due to its size and format, place the pamphlets and handbooks in the back pockets of the binder. Lastly, if you want to take your binder to the next level, use sheet protectors and tabs to identify the sections of the binder.

Overall, the information in your binder ensures that you and your children are able to get the best educational service and support because your documents are organized and easily accessible. In addition, you may have to refer back to what you actually agreed to and may have to review the protocols and procedures. So please don't throw anything away, especially if you signed the form confirming receipt of the document.

Establish School Connections

The week before school starts (before Open House), email your children's teachers to introduce yourself. This action demonstrates to the teachers that you are the empowered parent. In your introductory email, inform the teacher that you look forward to working with him/her, briefly describe the learning style and personality of your child that will aid in a smooth transition into his/her class, and provide your contact information (email address and phone number).

Similar to my documentation matters section, keep it very brief. There is no need for an essay.

Believe it or not, this one simple email will take you a long way. This initial connection builds rapport with your child's teacher. In addition, it sets the tone of mutual respect because you are initiating a home-school partnership. Lastly, you are establishing the communication norms, so if there is a need, the door is already open.

When you visit the school, take the time to connect with the other adults in the building. No, you don't have to invite them over for dinner but you need to at least become familiar with the faces and names of the adults in your child's school environment. Quiet as it's kept the janitors and secretaries know almost everything. I'm not talking about the formal structures and systems but the informal information. They know where all of the bodies are buried. In addition, they have information that you need to get things done. They see and hear everything. Also, you never know when you may need them to give you a helping hand.

For example, you miss a deadline for a school event. Although the event facilitator may have a hard date and tell you no. However, through your relationship with school secretary you discover that she will process the information and has the ability to add your form with hers. That's why it's so important to treat everyone with respect regardless of title or degree.

Yes, I am a very meticulous person and my process may sound like it's a lot. However, it works! Using these action steps will allow you to beat the crowds of procrastinating parents. In addition, you gain valuable ground because of the timing. Don't be a slowpoke, because like my momma said, the early bird gets the worm.

Chapter 7: Conclusion

You have read five chapters filled with a treasure chest of jewels to equip you as a parent in your school district's landscape. From understanding the players and their roles to the resources that they use in their game. In addition, you were introduced to the rules of engagement and the tactical strategies that are critical to winning a war. You are truly rich with wisdom! My hope is that after reading this playbook, you were able to learn new information and how to apply it in your children's school system.

The information in this book was not meant to create militant parents rioting outside of school board meetings. Rather to help position you inside of your school district's ecosystem so that you can advocate for your children. This vantage point allows you to take intentional and thoughtful measures to maneuver the perplexing ecosystem. My hope is that you will plant yourself in the middle of those critical conversations in your school district because your children will be the recipients of those decisions. Be the change that you want to see in your school district.

Run for your county's commissioner seat or Board of Education member because you are more than qualified. Your community needs your gifts and talents. Yes, you! I don't even know you or will probably never meet you but I believe in you. Why, because you are a parent. You have been blessed with the awesome responsibility to nurture and development human beings. Not only do you provide a home and food for your children, you meet their physical, emotional, social, and intellectual needs everyday, never missing a beat. Even when life got hard, something deep inside of you wouldn't allow you to quit. You kept pressing and fighting because you are a warrior. Your unique experiences and perspectives vital to your community. You don't need a college degree to have a voice.

May you be encouraged to act like an empowered parent and think like a school superintendent to ensure that you receive a high-quality education for your children. Ready, set, go!!!

ABOUT THE AUTHOR

Mary L. Young, Ed.D. has enjoyed a successful career in public education for more than 25 years. She is a proven leader having served as a School Superintendent, Executive Director, school administrator, and teacher. Her driving passion and vision is to empower others to reach their purpose. Dr. Young has been featured in national and local webinars, podcasts, and conferences.

Dr. Young's steadfast goal has always been to provide all students, regardless of their learning needs, race, ethnicity, or socioeconomic status, with options and choices upon graduation.

Through her experience and education, Dr. Young has developed a keen sense of effective leadership practices. She has had the opportunity to participate in the Harvard University's School Turnaround Leaders Institute, Harvard University's Urban School Leadership, Center for Creative Leadership Institute, and the New Leaders: D.C. School Leaders Network. In addition, she is a Principal Assessor for the National Association of Secondary Principals and certified Gallup Strengths Finders coach. Most recently, she graduated from the esteemed AASA Urban Superintendent Academy.

She has served as an adjunct professor at Trinity University & the University of Phoenix, and consultant for the D.C. Public Charter School Board & the Office of the State Superintendent of Education. In addition, she has held positions on the Board of Directors for Strategies to Empower People (STEP) and D.C. Association for Supervision and Curriculum Development (ASCD).

Dr. Young holds a Bachelor of Arts in Interdisciplinary Studies from the University of South Carolina, Masters of Education in Reading from Howard University and a Doctorate in Educational Administration and Policy from Howard University.

www.ingramcontent.com/pod-product-compliance
Lightning Source LLC
LaVergne TN
LVHW010608160826
845677LV00013B/3300